SUPERSTARS
of
PRO FOOTBALL

LARRY FITZGERALD

John Grabowski

Mason Crest Publishers

Produced by OTTN Publishing in association with
21st Century Publishing and Communications, Inc.

MASON CREST PUBLISHERS INC.
370 Reed Road
Broomall, Pennsylvania 19008
(866) MCP-BOOK (toll free)
www.masoncrest.com

Printed in the United States of America.

First Printing

9 8 7 6 5 4 3 2 1

Library of Congress Cataloging-in-Publication Data

Grabowski, John F.
  Larry Fitzgerald / John Grabowski.—1st printing.
     p. cm. — (Superstars of pro football)
  Includes bibliographical references.
  ISBN 978-1-4222-0549-5 (hardcover) — ISBN 978-1-4222-0822-9 (pbk.)
   1. Fitzgerald, Larry, 1983–   —Juvenile literature. 2. Football players—United
States—Biography—Juvenile literature. I. Title.
GV939.F55G73 2008
796.332092—dc22
[B]   2008024168

Publisher's note:
All quotations in this book come from original sources, and contain the spelling
and grammatical inconsistencies of the original text.

◀◀ CROSS-CURRENTS ▶▶

In the ebb and flow of the currents of life we are each influenced
by many people, places, and events that we directly experience or
have learned about. Throughout the chapters of this book you will
come across **CROSS-CURRENTS** reference bubbles. These bubbles
direct you to a **CROSS-CURRENTS** section in the back of the
book that contains fascinating and informative sidebars
and related pictures. Go on. ▶▶

◀◀CONTENTS▶▶

A GLORIOUS SEASON

Larry Fitzgerald did not need an extra reason to do well in his sophomore season playing football for the University of Pittsburgh Panthers. He had a successful freshman year playing wide receiver, and the future looked bright. The memory of his late mother, however, inspired Larry to a new level of dedication. He was not playing just for himself.

A Family Tragedy

Tragedy had struck the Fitzgerald household the previous spring. Larry's mother, Carol, passed away at age 37 after a long battle with breast cancer. Her death hit Larry especially hard. He was

Pittsburgh Panthers receiver Larry Fitzgerald gallops away from a Boston College defender for a 58-yard gain, November 1, 2003. In the game, which Pitt won by a score of 24-13, Larry broke the NCAA record for most consecutive games with a touchdown reception.

close to both of his parents and regularly called home to Minneapolis while away at school.

Many people would have understood if Larry had become depressed and put football and his other interests aside. He was determined, however, not let that happen. He kept thinking about the lessons his mother had taught him and the values he had been taught since he was a young child. He knew his mother would want him to finish what he started, to be the best he could be, and to be a good person. He was determined to follow his mother's lessons. As he told Joe Bendel of the *Pittsburgh Tribune-Review*,

> **"I've dedicated the rest of my life to her, not just this football season. I'm conscious of everything I do. I'm living the way that would make her happy, trying to be the man she raised me to be."**

Larry threw himself into his training program for football. He lifted weights, ran drills, caught passes, and watched films of past games. He added 15 pounds of muscle and dropped his body fat from 6 percent to 4 percent. By the time the new season started in September, Larry was ready to show the football world what he could do.

Leading the Panthers

The Panthers opened their season against the Kent State Golden Flashes. Larry caught six passes for 123 yards as the Panthers defeated the Golden Flashes, 43-3. Three of his catches went for **touchdowns**. It was an emotional day for Larry, whose thoughts were often with his mother. As he told Doug Frattallone of the *Minnesota Score*,

> **"I thought about her quite frequently while I was out there. But I had to take care of business. It was really difficult at times, but I also have an obligation to my teammates and my coaches to perform at a level they expect."**

The rest of Larry's sophomore season was filled with similar performances. He set seven Big East Conference receiving records, including single-season receiving yards, **receptions**, and touchdown catches. Coaches and scouts who saw him play were impressed with his talent. Notre Dame head coach Tyrone Willingham had this to say about Larry's ability as a receiver in heavy coverage:

> **"This guy is really unbelievable. He's doing some great things. I watched one of his highlights and as a coach you say, 'Don't you dare throw the ball! He's triple covered!' And it's like he's the only guy there because he comes away with it being triple covered."**

Larry Fitzgerald is congratulated by Pitt teammates after scoring a touchdown against Texas A&M, College Station, Texas, September 27, 2003. Pitt won the game, 37-26.

Unfortunately, Larry's brilliant sophomore season ended in disappointment. With a record of eight wins and three losses heading into their last game, the Panthers had a chance to win a share of the Big East championship and an invitation to a Bowl Championship Series (BCS) game. Both hopes disappeared as the Panthers lost the season's last game to the University of Miami by a score of 28-14. Panthers **quarterback** Rod Rutherford was **sacked** nine times by the Hurricanes' defense. He only completed three passes to Larry for a total of 26 yards. One of these passes, however, went for a touchdown. That pass extended Larry's National Collegiate Athletic Association (NCAA) record streak to 18 games in a row with a scoring catch.

Larry Fitzgerald (center) holds the Biletnikoff Award, given each year to the best college receiver in the nation, December 11, 2003. Joining him at the 2003 College Football Awards ceremony are Pitt head coach Walt Harris (left) and offensive coordinator J. D. Brookhart.

The season's last game might have cost Larry his shot at the Heisman Trophy, college football's most prestigious award. Although no sophomore had ever won the Heisman, Larry had been mentioned all season as one of the top candidates for the award. When the Heisman vote was announced in December, Larry was edged out by University of Oklahoma quarterback Pat White.

CROSS-CURRENTS
To learn about a key figure in the development of Larry's favorite sport, read "The Father of American Football." Go to page 46. ▶▶

Records and Awards

Larry finished his sophomore season at Pitt with 87 receptions for 1,595 yards and 22 touchdowns. After just two seasons, his name was already high on the list of all-time Panther receiving greats. In 26 college games, he had caught 161 passes for 2,677 yards and 34 touchdowns. Only Lateef Grim (178) and Antonio Bryant (173) had more receptions; only Bryant (3,061), Dietrich Jells (3,003), and Grim (2,680) had more total yards receiving. Each of those three players, however, had played at least three seasons for the Panthers. Larry also set a school record with 14 games of at least 100 yards receiving. In addition, he became the first Panther to record back-to-back seasons with 1,000 yards receiving.

In recognition of his performance, Larry was named to all the major All-American teams and cited as the Eastern College Athletic Conference Division I-A Player of the Year. Praise and awards continued to come his way. He received the Chic Harley Award as the Touchdown Club of Columbus Player of the Year, as well as the Biletnikoff Award as the nation's top college-football receiver.

CROSS-CURRENTS
Read "Fred Biletnikoff" to learn about the former star player for whom a major college award is named. Go to page 47. ▶▶

Larry's crowning achievement came in mid-December. He was awarded the Walter Camp Award as the nation's top college football player. The winner of the Walter Camp Award is chosen by the NCAA Division I-A coaches and sports information directors. No sophomore had ever taken the prize since it was first awarded in 1967.

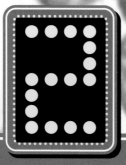

A SOLID FOUNDATION

Larry Darnell Fitzgerald Jr. was born on August 31, 1983, in Minneapolis, Minnesota. He was the first child of Larry and Carol Fitzgerald. His brother Marcus was born three years later. Larry Sr. is the sports editor of the *Minnesota Spokesman-Recorder* and the host of a radio sports program. His wife worked for the Minnesota Department of Health.

Developing a Talent

Larry Sr. had been an outstanding lineman at Indiana State University during his college days. His sons inherited his love for football. Larry Jr. played touch football until middle school.

Born in Minneapolis in 1983, Larry Fitzgerald grew up a huge football fan. While in high school, Larry got the chance to serve as ball boy for the Minnesota Vikings.

During his high school years, Larry's football education received an unexpected boost. His father had been cohosting a radio sports talk show with Minnesota Vikings head coach Dennis Green. Through Green, Larry Jr. had the chance to become a ball boy for the Vikings.

Larry watched and talked to Vikings All-Pro receivers Cris Carter and Randy Moss every chance he got. It was a great learning experience for him. As he told Jon Krawczynski of the Associated Press,

CROSS-CURRENTS

If you would like to learn more about the newspaper where Larry's father works, read "The Minnesota Spokesman-Recorder." *Go to page 48.* ▶▶

❝Just watching guys like Cris Carter, Jake Reed, and Randy Moss and guys like that growing up, working so hard in practice every day to make themselves the great players they are, and were, for the Vikings when they were in their heyday. I think it gave me a little appreciation for how much hard work it took to be great.**❞**

Larry first attended Minnehaha Academy and then transferred to the Academy of Holy Angels for his sophomore year of high school. While there, Larry was a star on the football field. His schoolwork, however, suffered. Larry had a lot to worry about: his mother had been diagnosed with breast cancer. His poor grades scared some colleges away, and Larry's hopes of receiving a scholarship to a top school faded.

University of Pittsburgh coach Walt Harris was one of several people who suggested that he transfer to a prep school. Following this advice, Larry left Holy Angels in the middle of his senior year and enrolled at Valley Forge Military Academy, in Pennsylvania. He worked hard and graduated one-and-a-half years later. In the fall of 2002, he began classes at the University of Pittsburgh—with a scholarship.

The Making of a Star

Larry possessed an exceptionally strong pair of hands and the ability to stay focused under pressure. It was almost impossible to tear the ball away from him once he got hold of it.

In a mid-November game against the West Virginia University Mountaineers, Larry was hit hard by cornerback Adam "Pacman" Jones just after he caught the ball. Mountaineers **safety** Brian King came over to help and smacked the ball with his hand. The referees signaled Jones for **pass interference**, but Larry somehow managed to hold onto the ball. King later told Tim Layden in a *Sports Illustrated* article,

❝I hit the ball hard and [Pacman] got called for pass interference and he still caught the ball. I looked at Pac-Man and said, 'We've got no answers for this guy.'**❞**

Minnesota Vikings wide receiver Randy Moss fends off a Detroit Lions tackler, 1998. Larry Fitzgerald's time as a ball boy for the Vikings gave him a chance to see great receivers like Moss, Cris Carter, and Jake Reed up close.

Freshman Season Finale

Larry had a solid freshman year for the Panthers, catching 69 passes for 1,005 yards and 12 touchdowns. For his performance, he was named to the All-Big East team.

Larry's freshman year ended with the Insight Bowl against the Oregon State Beavers. Three minutes into the game, he made a play that had everyone talking. With the Panthers on the Beavers' 40-yard line, quarterback Rod Rutherford dropped

CROSS-CURRENTS

Read "The First All-America Team" to learn about the origins of this honor for college football players. Go to page 48. ▶▶

In action from September 27, 2003, Texas A&M defensive back Sean Weston is draped all over Larry Fitzgerald—and even has a hand on his face mask—but Larry has the concentration to pull down the pass.

back to pass. Larry raced past Beavers safety Mitch Meeuwsen toward the **end zone**. Rutherford threw a pass that appeared to be beyond Larry's reach. Running at full speed, Larry leaped forward. With his arms outstretched and his body parallel to the ground, he caught the ball a split second before hitting the ground. Incredibly, he managed to hold onto it for a touchdown. It was the Panthers' first touchdown on their way to a 38-13 victory.

Tragedy

The following April, Larry was at school when he received a call from his father, telling him to come home as quickly as possible. His mother was not doing well. Larry flew home to find his mother on a respirator in a local hospital. The cancer had spread to her lungs and brain.

While she was waiting to undergo surgery to relieve the swelling in her skull, she took a turn for the worse. Larry was understandably upset. His mother's condition failed to improve, and doctors said there was no hope for recovery. She passed away a few days later.

Accepting his mother's death was the hardest thing Larry ever had to do. Making matters even worse, Larry and his mother had a disagreement the last time he saw her. In a *Sports Illustrated* article, his father talked about how he tried to console Larry:

> **"He was so overwhelmed with grief because they never patched things up. I told him, 'Don't you carry that with you, Larry. Your mother loved you and you loved her. Don't take any other feelings out of this room today.'"**

Larry would never forget the lessons his mother taught him. He kept her driver's license in his wallet so that a part of her would always be with him. He decided to dedicate his life to his mother and to be the kind of person she had raised him to be. With his mother in mind, Larry returned to Pittsburgh and began preparing for his sophomore season.

WELCOME TO THE NFL

After his outstanding sophomore year playing for the University of Pittsburgh Panthers, it was no surprise that Larry started thinking seriously about playing in the National Football League (NFL). Most observers believed he would definitely be selected as one of the first ten picks if he were to enter the league's draft.

Walt Harris, Larry's coach at the University of Pittsburgh, was supportive of his star player. As he told Joe Bendel of the *Pittsburgh Tribune-Review*,

❝He not only showed people how to make catches, but showed a respect for the game. I have witnessed

video of high school games when people make a play and hand the ball to the official [like Fitzgerald does after scores]. I think he's had a tremendous effect on our program and on players around the country. **"**

Challenging a Rule

The only thing that seemed to stand between Larry and the NFL was a league rule about a player's age. According to NFL rules, a player is not eligible for the league's draft until three years after he graduated from high school. The purpose of the rule is to ensure that a player is mature enough, both physically and mentally, to handle the demands of playing in the league.

After his sophomore season at the University of Pittsburgh, Larry Fitzgerald decided to turn professional. In the 2004 NFL draft, he was selected by the Arizona Cardinals with the third overall pick.

As Jeff Pash, chief counsel for the league, explained in a conference call with reporters,

"It is perfectly clear that players that stay in school are better players and have more lucrative careers. The people who will be hurt are the players who, one way or another, try to make the jump and are not ready to do so, and they lose their eligibility and their scholarship and their opportunity to play in the NFL. It's not a good thing for us, but we are not the primary loser."

In September 2003, Maurice Clarett, a sophomore running back from Ohio State University, filed a lawsuit against the NFL in an attempt to overturn this rule. Although Larry had graduated in May 2002—only two years before the 2004 NFL draft—he, too, decided to apply to become eligible for the draft. He asked the league to give him a special exemption from the rule. He had, after all, transferred to Valley Forge Military Academy in the middle of his senior year and spent a fifth year in high school rather than the usual four. The way Larry and his family looked at it, he had played for three years since his original high school class had graduated.

On February 5, 2004, a United States District Court judge in New York City struck down the league's rule in Clarett's suit. The NFL announced that it would appeal the ruling, but it also said that it had granted Larry's request for a special exemption. His path to the NFL had been cleared.

The 2004 NFL Draft

Scouts usually rate receivers entering the NFL draft in five categories: hands, patterns, run after the catch, release (getting away quickly from the line of scrimmage), and blocking. The network of scouts, correspondents, and former college and pro coaches that makes up *The Sporting News* Pro Football War Room grade prospects in each of those categories on a scale from 1.0 to 9.0. They gave Larry grades of 9.0 in hands, patterns, and blocking; an 8.7 in run after the catch; and an 8.6 in release. Players rating between 7.0 and 8.0 are considered "potential **Pro Bowl** players."

Talented but troubled Ohio State University running back Maurice Clarett carries the ball against San Jose State in a 2002 game. Clarett challenged the NFL's rule that players could not be drafted until three years after they had graduated from high school.

Anyone with a score over 8.0 is considered a future "franchise player." Larry's final overall grade was an incredible 8.9.

It was no surprise, then, that Larry was the first wide receiver selected in the 2004 NFL draft. The draft was held at Madison Square Garden, in New York City, on April 24. The Arizona Cardinals held the third overall pick. The San Diego Chargers selected University of Mississippi quarterback Eli Manning with the first pick

CROSS-CURRENTS

To learn about other Pitt graduates who have become pro football players, read "Pittsburgh Panthers in the NFL." Go to page 50. ▶▶

and then traded him to the New York Giants. The Oakland Raiders took University of Iowa offensive tackle Robert Gallery next. When it came time for the Cardinals to choose, NFL commissioner Paul Tagliabue approached the microphone, and said:

"With the third pick of the NFL Draft, the Arizona Cardinals select wide receiver Larry Fitzgerald from the University of Pittsburgh."

University of Iowa offensive tackle Robert Gallery (left) chats with SIRIUS Satellite Radio host Phil Simms at the NFL draft headquarters at Madison Square Garden in New York, April 24, 2004. Gallery and University of Mississippi quarterback Eli Manning were the only players drafted ahead of Larry Fitzgerald.

Larry was thrilled to have been picked by Arizona, which had recently hired his old family friend, Dennis Green, as its coach. He explained to his father,

"To be able to come and play for Coach Green is an honor. I'm familiar with his coaching staff, and when you feel comfortable, usually that makes everything else a lot easier, because you prepare easier."

The First Contract

At the beginning of August, Larry signed his first pro contract. It was a six-year deal that could earn him as much as $60 million. Under the contract, some of the money Larry could earn was in the form of escalators. An escalator is part of a contract that says a player will be paid a certain amount for reaching a certain level of performance. A running back, for example, might have an escalator that pays him extra money if he reaches 2,000 yards rushing in a season.

Teams include escalators in contracts for several reasons. One reason is that escalators allow them to fit a large contract under the salary cap (the limit on the amount of money a team can pay its players). Teams also use escalators to help them get out of a big contract if a player fails to live up to expectations.

On the other hand, if a player reaches the escalators, he will probably expect a much higher salary under his next contract. According to the NFL Players Association, Larry's contract contained at least $35 million in escalators. Cardinals general manager Rod Graves said the team intended to redo Larry's contract after four years if he reached his escalators.

An Impressive Rookie Year

The Cardinals are charter members of the NFL and the oldest continuously run professional football franchise in the country. In recent years, they have been one of the least successful teams in the league. The Cardinals had finished in last place in their division in the four previous seasons before 2004, never winning more than five games in a season. In 2003, they became just the second team in the past 30 years to finish last in the league in both points scored and points allowed.

Many people thought the Cardinals might improve in the 2004 season because the team had hired Dennis Green. Green had a proven track record, having led the Minnesota Vikings to the **playoffs** in 8 of his 10 seasons as the team's head coach. Also, the Cardinals had Anquan Boldin, a star receiver who caught 101 passes as a **rookie** in 2003. Green hoped Larry would team with Boldin to give the Cardinals one of the top pass-catching duos in the league. Fans hoped the pair would give the Cardinals much-needed scoring power.

CROSS-CURRENTS

For more on the Fitzgerald family friend hired to coach the Cardinals in 2004, read "Head Coach Dennis Green." Go to page 50. ▶▶

Larry made his professional debut in the Cardinals' first preseason game against the Minnesota Vikings, on August 14. Playing in front of his family and hometown fans, he was understandably nervous. Toward the end of the first period, he caught a five-yard pass from quarterback Josh McCown. Unfortunately, he also sprained his ankle, cutting short his debut. The Cardinals lost by a score of 23-6.

The Cardinals began the regular season in St. Louis, Missouri, with a game against the St. Louis Rams. Larry's ankle was feeling much better. He had an impressive regular-season debut, catching four passes for 70 yards—more than anyone else on his team. More than half of those yards came on a **flea-flicker** from McCown barely one minute into the game. Unfortunately, with Boldin sidelined with an injury, the Cardinals could not keep up much of an attack. They lost to the Rams, 17-10. It was the team's 14th loss in a row on the road.

The Cardinals' offense continued to struggle in the next two games before coming alive with a 34-10 win over the New Orleans Saints. The next week, while playing against the San Francisco 49ers, Larry scored his first NFL touchdown on a 35-yard pass from McCown. Larry's touchdown gave the Cardinals a 20-12 lead with under eight minutes left to play. The 49ers, however, tied the game and went on to beat the Cardinals in **overtime**.

A Fast Learner

Many rookies begin their pro careers as reserves, learning as they watch the veterans play the game. As they learn the pro game, they

The Arizona Cardinals run onto the field before a home game. In 2004, new head coach Dennis Green hoped that rookie Larry Fitzgerald and second-year man Anquan Boldin would form a potent receiving duo.

With San Francisco 49ers linebacker Jeff Ulbrich trying to defend him, Larry Fitzgerald leaps high for a catch, October 10, 2004. Larry caught five passes for 94 yards and a touchdown on the day, but the 49ers handed the Cardinals a 31-28 loss.

earn more and more playing time. Eventually, some of them become starting players.

Larry did not have the luxury of taking things slowly. As the third overall pick in the draft, he found that much was expected of him right from the start. Luckily, he was a fast learner. He made the transition from college All-America to NFL starter with ease. As Larry told Judy Battista of *The New York Times*,

> **"They threw me in the fire fast and everybody was moving so fast. Every week, you're playing against great players. . . . My route-running has gotten so much better. In college, you run your route. Now, I know everything conceptually. I know what the opposite receiver is doing. I understand the coverages presnap."**

Larry played an important role in Arizona's 24-23 win over the Miami Dolphins in the ninth week of the season. He caught a 48-yard pass from McCown with just over one minute remaining in the game. Four plays later, he caught a two-yard toss to tie the score. After they made the extra point, the Cardinals' losing streak on the road—which had reached 17 games—was over.

Larry continued to improve during the second half of the season. He caught a season-high seven passes against the Carolina Panthers and had a pair of touchdown catches against both the Rams and the Seattle Seahawks. The Cardinals, however, continued to lose games. The team finished the season with a record of 6-10. At least that record was good enough to get them out of last place in the National Football Conference (NFC) West Division. The woeful San Francisco 49ers finished with an even-worse record of 2-14.

SUCCESS AND DISAPPOINTMENT

Although they did not live up to expectations, Larry's team showed improvement in 2004. They lost far more than they won, but they lost only by an average of about 10 points per game—down from about 20 points. The Cardinals' receivers—Larry, Boldin, and Bryant Johnson—showed great promise, and the team was optimistic about the upcoming 2005 season.

Changes on the Cardinals

In order to improve the team's offense, two-time Most Valuable Player (MVP) Kurt Warner was signed to play quarterback.

Larry Fitzgerald takes a ride with Minnie Mouse during the ESPN Weekend at Disney MGM Studios, Orlando, Florida, February 26, 2005. Larry had provided a few highlights during his rookie season, and Cardinals fans looked for him to have a breakout year in 2005.

Warner was no longer at the top of his career, but Green hoped he would provide the club with leadership and stability. The team expected rookies Marcel Shipp and J.J. Arrington to improve its running game, so Arizona's prospects seemed bright. Several writers, in fact, picked Arizona to win the NFC West Division championship.

Unfortunately, things did not go as planned for the Cardinals. The team won three of its four preseason games in 2005. Once the regular season began, however, the team fell back into its losing ways. The Cardinals lost their first three games by a total of 53 points. Larry started the year with an outstanding game against

CROSS-CURRENTS

To learn about a game Larry played in Mexico during 2005, read "NFL Football Around the World." Go to page 52. ▶▶

the New York Giants. He caught 13 passes for 155 yards—both career highs. The Cardinals' defense, however, left much to be desired. The Giants scored an easy 42-19 win.

Larry gained 102 yards in the Cardinals' first victory of the season, a 31-14 win over the 49ers. The next week he again had a big game, with 136 yards gained against the Carolina Panthers. Anquan Boldin, who had missed six games in 2004 with an injury to his right knee, also had more than 100 yards receiving in each of these games. It was the first time an NFL team had two wide receivers each gain more than 100 yards in back-to-back games since the Tennessee Titans' Kevin Dyson and Derrick Mason had done it in 2001.

Personal Success

Larry continued to shine throughout the rest of the season. He had four more games with 100 or more yards receiving, giving him a total of seven for the year. With his first reception of the day against San Francisco on December 4, he surpassed 1,000 receiving yards for the year.

On New Year's Day the Cardinals traveled to Indianapolis to play the Colts in their last regular-season game. They battled the playoff-bound Colts, but lost by a score of 17-13. It was, however, another big game for Larry. He caught six passes, giving him an incredible 103 receptions for the year. At 22 years old, he became the youngest player in NFL history to catch more than 100 passes in a season. Larry's 103 catches were a new team record, and tied the Carolina Panthers' Steve Smith for the league lead. Larry's 1,409 receiving yards also set a Cardinals record.

Boldin also reached the 100-catch mark in the same game. Larry and Boldin became just the third pair of teammates to each make 100 receptions in the same season. The previous pairs were the Detroit Lions' Herman Moore and Brett Perriman, in 1995, and the Denver Broncos' Rod Smith and Ed McCaffrey, in 2000.

Larry's tremendous second NFL season was capped by his selection for the Pro Bowl. The Pro Bowl game—which is played each year in Honolulu, Hawaii, on the Sunday after the Super Bowl—matches the best players from the NFL's two conferences, the NFC and the American Football Conference (AFC). Larry was proud to be chosen for the Pro Bowl in only his second year in the league. Always looking for ways to improve himself, he made the most of this opportunity to play with—and against—the best players in the league. As reported by Kate Brandt on the Cardinals' Web site, Larry explained,

> **❝I'm always in their ear. They try to get away from me. I'm always ready and willing to learn some new things from anybody that is willing to give it to me. It's an honor to be here and all of these guys are really cool.❞**

Larry Fitzgerald leaps to make a catch against the Indianapolis Colts, January 1, 2006. The Colts won the New Year's Day matchup, 17-13, but Larry became the youngest player in NFL history to get 100 receptions in a single season.

Early in the second quarter of the Pro Bowl, Larry caught a pass and ran for 12 yards before being pulled down. Three plays later, he was on the receiving end of a 32-yard pass from quarterback Michael Vick. It was the longest play of the game. The victorious NFC squad beat the AFC by a score of 23-17.

Larry Fitzgerald grapples with safety Bob Sanders of the Indianapolis Colts during the 2006 Pro Bowl. Larry, who had tied for the league lead in receiving yards, was voted to the Pro Bowl in just his second season.

Renewed Optimism

The Cardinals' hopes for improvement in the 2006 season were based on two headline-grabbing additions to the team. First, Indianapolis Colts All-Pro running back Edgerrin James joined the team as a **free agent**, signing a four-year, $30 million contract in March. He was expected to improve the team's rushing attack, which had been the worst in the league in 2005. The next month the Cardinals drafted All-America quarterback Matt Leinart of the University of Southern California, with the tenth overall pick. Although Leinart was not expected to take over the position from Kurt Warner immediately, he would be the Cardinals' quarterback of the future. With Larry and Boldin anchoring the league's best passing offense, Arizona looked set to improve.

The Cardinals' hopes were high for another reason as well. University of Phoenix Stadium, the Cardinals' new $455 million home, was ready to open in Glendale, Arizona. With its retractable roof, fans and players alike were excited about the new stadium. After three years of construction, the 63,400-seat stadium was ready for the Cardinals' first preseason game on August 12, 2006. In the first game played in the new stadium, the Cardinals defeated the Pittsburgh Steelers, 21-13.

The opening game of the regular season was also a success. Playing in front of a sellout crowd, the Cardinals beat the 49ers, 34-27. Larry caught a team-high nine passes from Warner to gain 133 yards.

Sitting Out

Unfortunately, things quickly began to unravel for Larry's team. The Cardinals traveled to Seattle, where they lost, 21-10, to the Seahawks in the second week of the regular season. The Seahawks broke Larry's streak of six 100-yard-receiving games against NFC West teams as they held him to four catches for 52 yards. Losses to the St. Louis Rams and the Atlanta Falcons dropped the Cardinals to a 1-3 record after the first month of the season. Coach Green was unhappy with Warner's performance and announced that Leinart would start at quarterback in the Cardinals' next game, against the Kansas City Chiefs.

Leinart got off to a good start, throwing two touchdown passes in the first quarter. The second was a five-yard pass to Larry to give their team a 14-0 lead. Later that quarter, however, Larry felt a pop in his **hamstring** while he was running. He was forced to leave the game, which the Chiefs came back to win, 23-20. Doctors found a small tear in his hamstring. The injury was bad enough to keep Larry sidelined for nearly a month.

CROSS-CURRENTS

Check out "Football Injuries" to learn about the many ways in which players can be hurt during games. Go to page 53. ▶▶

The Cardinals lost all three games that Larry missed. Their October 16th loss to the undefeated Chicago Bears was especially frustrating. Although the Cardinals were winning 20-0 at halftime, the Bears came back to beat them, 24-23. Coach Green stormed out of the postgame press conference, furious about the Cardinals' loss.

Larry returned to action on November 12, 2006, against the Dallas Cowboys. His return, unfortunately, did not help the Cardinals break their losing streak. Although Larry caught six passes for 80 yards, the team lost, 27-10—its eighth straight defeat.

In spite of his team's disappointing record, Larry had several bright moments over the final weeks of the season. The November 26 game against the Minnesota Vikings was his first regular-season game back in his hometown. His only previous appearance in Minnesota as a pro had been during the 2004 preseason game in which he injured his ankle early in the game. Larry was anxious to make things different this time around. As he told Jon Krawczynski of the Associated Press,

❝This is my third year now. . . . I'm a lot more mature. I have a lot better understanding of what my role is on this team, what my job is. I just need to go out there and relax and have a good time and help my ballclub win.❞

Larry played one of his best games as a pro that day. He caught 11 passes for a career-high 172 yards. Unfortunately, it was not enough to carry the Cardinals to victory. The Vikings hung on for a 31-26 win.

Three weeks later, Larry caught five passes for 77 yards in a 37-20 loss to the Denver Broncos. In that game he achieved another milestone: more than 3,000 yards in receiving yardage for his career. The

Larry Fitzgerald and Minnesota Vikings cornerback Cedric Griffin battle for a ball at the Metrodome in Minneapolis, November 26, 2006. Larry was fabulous in his first regular-season game in his hometown—he caught 11 passes for 172 yards—but the Vikings won, 31-26.

Larry Fitzgerald drags Rams cornerback Tye Hill into the end zone for a touchdown during Arizona's December 3, 2006, game against St. Louis. The Cardinals won, 34-20. But this and Arizona's four other wins in 2006 weren't enough to save head coach Dennis Green's job.

following week, he set another personal record with a 57-yard catch against the 49ers.

Larry finished the 2006 season with 69 catches. Even though he had missed three weeks with an injury, he came up just 54 yards short of a second 1,000-yard season.

The Cardinals bounced back to win four of the season's last seven games. This was not enough, however, to save Green's job. The day after the team's season-ending 27-20 defeat by the San Diego Chargers, the coach was fired. As reported by Kent Somers of *The Arizona Republic*, Cardinals vice president Michael Bidwill explained,

> **In the final analysis, when you look at the three years of wins and losses, we didn't win enough games. I think Dennis Green understands that in this league you've got to win games. We're all sorry it didn't turn out.**

The players for the most part were disappointed with the firing. According to Jim Gintonio of *The Arizona Republic*, linebacker Orlando Huff said,

> **Dennis is a good coach, a great person, a great motivator. I mean, you can't blame all this on Denny, what's going on. He's been there. He hasn't put guys [down] in the media. All he asks you [for] is hard work, come to work and focus. You can't blame none of this on Denny, that's my take, because he did his job.**

With a record of 16-32 in the three previous seasons, and just one winning season over the previous 21 years, the Cardinals began the search for a new head coach.

CARRYING ON THE FIGHT

L arry's first three years on the Arizona Cardinals were guided by head coach Dennis Green. Green was not only his coach, but also a friend of his family. The coach's departure left a void that would be difficult to fill. How Larry reacted to the firing of Green had a large impact on the team's hopes for the future.

A New Start

The search for the Cardinals' new head coach ended in mid-January 2007, when the team signed Ken Whisenhunt to a four-year contract. In the past, Whisenhunt had played tight end for the Atlanta Falcons, and he had also been offensive

Larry Fitzgerald tosses a football around on a sandlot baseball field in Phoenix. As the 2007 season approached, rumors surfaced that Larry wasn't happy with the hiring of new Cardinals head coach Ken Whisenhunt.

coordinator for the Pittsburgh Steelers. An *ESPN.com* article reported Whisenhunt expressing his goals for the team:

> **"We're not going to change the world. That's not the goal, guys, let's face it. But I think we can change enough things, and pretty quickly, to make good progress in a short time. I know we can change some attitudes. And I think, from talking to most of the [veterans], they're anxious to get started."**

Larry was still upset about the firing of Dennis Green. Rumors spread that he was not happy with the hiring of Whisenhunt. It did not take long, however, before the new coach won Larry over. The Associated Press reported Larry's description of his new coach and staff:

> **"[They are] high-character guys who have been straight up with me from Day One. . . . Everything you get you have to earn, and I like that."**

Turning the Corner

Although the Cardinals were winless in the 2007 preseason, the team's hopes were high as Arizona began the regular season. The team's first game was against the San Francisco 49ers, and it was broadcast on *Monday Night Football.* Larry struggled in the opening game, catching just three passes for 20 yards amid swirling winds. In spite of Larry's struggle, the Cardinals led 17-13 with less than three minutes left to play. The 49ers did not give up, however. They scored a touchdown with just 26 seconds left on the clock to defeat the Cardinals.

The opening loss did not break the team's spirit. In their next game, against the Seattle Seahawks, the Cardinals led 17-0, lost the lead, and then came back to win the game. Larry led the team with seven catches for 87 yards. When kicker Neil Rackers made a 42-yard field goal with four seconds left to play, Whisenhunt had recorded his first victory as a head coach.

The Cardinals won two more times over the next three weeks, and Larry continued to shine. He had an especially good game in the Cardinals' 21-14 win over Pittsburgh, with 11 catches for 123 yards.

The Cardinals' record stood at 5-5 when they played San Francisco again on November 25. Although Arizona lost in overtime, Larry had a great game, catching nine passes for 156 yards. Forty-eight of those yards came when Larry caught Kurt Warner's last-second pass into the end zone at the end of the first half. This touchdown catch was Larry's second of the game and the 30th of his career. In this game, Larry also exceeded 1,000-yards receiving in one season for the

Larry Fitzgerald recovers an onside kick attempted by the St. Louis Rams, October 7, 2007. With nine receptions for 136 yards and a touchdown, Larry led the Cardinals to a 34-31 victory in the game.

Larry Fitzgerald catches a pass during practice for the 2008 Pro Bowl. With 100 receptions, 10 touchdowns, and more than 1,400 receiving yards during the 2007 season, Larry was voted a Pro Bowl starter for the NFC.

second time in his career. Incredibly, he performed these feats while suffering from a groin injury.

The injury kept Larry out of the Cardinals' game against the Cleveland Browns the following week. He returned for the final four games of the season. In the last game of the year, he ended another magnificent season with 11 catches for 171 yards and two touchdowns, as the Cardinals beat the St. Louis Rams, 48-19.

The Cardinals finished the 2007 season with an 8-8 record—their best record since 1998. Larry had 100 catches for the second time, and he matched the 1,409 receiving yards that he had gained in 2005. He was rewarded for his efforts with his second Pro Bowl selection, this time as a starter for the NFC.

The Pro Bowl game ended Larry's season on a high note, as he scored the NFC's opening touchdown. This helped the NFC team win the game, 42-30. After three years of losing seasons, the Cardinals at last appeared to be headed in the right direction. At the age of 24, Larry's future looked bright.

CROSS-CURRENTS

Read "The Receptions Record" to learn about the NFL players who have caught the most passes in a single season. Go to page 54. ▶▶

Contract Negotiations

Larry's future as a Cardinal, however, depended on his contract. In order to keep players' salaries from increasing at an excessive rate, NFL team owners had set a salary cap in 1994. The salary cap is a set amount of money that teams are allowed to spend on all player salaries for a particular year. The salary cap for 2008 was about $116.7 million per team. That figure is determined by dividing a percentage of the league's projected total revenues by the number of teams in the league.

The salary cap creates challenges for some teams. If a team has several star players earning large salaries, it might not have enough money to pay its other players well. After these other players have been in the league for a few years, they can become free agents. This allows them to join another team that can afford to pay them more.

Teams often try to get around the limitations of the salary cap by giving a signing bonus when a player signs a new contract. The signing bonus guarantees the player a large amount of money, which is beneficial to the player. This way, the player's annual salary can be lower, to help the team stay under the salary cap.

After Larry's outstanding 2007 season—his fourth with the team—the Cardinals tried to renegotiate his contract. Because Larry had qualified for the escalators in his original contract, the Cardinals had to pay him $14.6 million in 2008 and $17.4 million in 2009. Under the league's salary cap, that was an exceptional amount of money to pay one player. If he played out those final two years of his contract, however, he would become an unrestricted free agent, able to earn even more with another team.

Negotiations between the Cardinals and Larry's agent, Eugene Parker, went slowly. The Cardinals offered Larry $25 million guaranteed for four years. That would make him the highest-paid receiver in the league. Larry, however, wanted more than the $32.5 million that had been guaranteed to Calvin Johnson of the Detroit Lions. The Cardinals argued that Johnson's contract had been for six years while Fitzgerald wanted a four-year deal. The negotiations dragged on, with no end in sight.

Trade Rumors

While negotiations between Larry and the Cardinals moved slowly, rumors began that the Cardinals were trying to trade him to another team. The Cardinals denied this rumor, saying that Larry would remain with the team, but it did not stop people from talking.

One rumor was that Larry would be traded to the Minnesota Vikings. The Vikings had expressed interest in Larry as far back as the beginning of the 2007 season. They were in desperate need of a wide receiver. According to the rumor, Larry would be traded to the Vikings in exchange for the seventh overall draft and one or two other players. If it happened, the trade would send Larry back to his home state.

CROSS-CURRENTS

If you would like to read about the biggest trade in Cardinals history, check out "The Ollie Matson Trade." Go to page 55. ▶▶

The other rumor was more of a long shot. The Philadelphia Eagles were trying to acquire free-agent cornerback Asante Samuel of the New England Patriots. If they could get Samuel, they would give the Cardinals cornerback Lito Shepard and the 19th pick in the draft in exchange for Larry. Both of these rumors, however, proved to be nothing more than talk.

A New Deal

Larry and the Cardinals finally agreed on a new deal in March of 2008. The four-year contract is worth $40 million, with about $30 million guaranteed. It includes a $15 million signing bonus and an additional $5 million in bonus money in 2009.

Because the contract is for just four years, Larry will be 28 years old when it ends. As long as he is not seriously injured, he will still be young enough to sign another contract for a lot of money.

The Cardinals benefited from the deal as well. With much of Larry's money paid in bonuses rather than salary, the team saved

Larry Fitzgerald talks to the media. After the 2007 season, Larry and the Cardinals entered drawn-out contract negotiations, and there were even rumors that the team might be looking to trade the star receiver.

In March 2008, Larry Fitzgerald signed a four-year deal with Arizona—ensuring that the spectacularly gifted wide receiver will entertain and excite Cardinals fans for many games to come.

nearly $9 million in salary cap space. This left the team more money to spend on free agents who could help strengthen the team.

A Look Into the Future

In the 2008 NFL draft, the Cardinals picked cornerback Dominique Rodgers-Cromartie from Tennessee State University in hopes of improving their defensive team. The young player was happy to join a team with Pro Bowlers like Larry and Anquan Boldin on offense. He knew that playing against them in practice would only make him a better player. As Darren Urban reported Rodgers-Cromartie saying on the Cardinals' Web site,

> **"That's one of the first things I thought about when they told me. I was like, 'Man, I've got the best.'"**

Many people think the best will only get better. As the highest-paid player in the league who is not a quarterback, Larry is expected to remain one of the top players in the NFL. Both fans and management will be carefully watching his every move. Many athletes have signed big contracts and then failed to perform well. Sometimes, highly paid players do not play well because they think they have "made it" and do not have to try as hard as they did before.

With Larry's upbringing, it is unlikely that he will stop working hard. His mother, Carol, is still his guiding light, giving him internal strength. As he once told Mark Craig of the *Star Tribune*,

> **"My mom wouldn't want me complaining and doing all that other stuff you see around the league. Wait. No, she wouldn't *let* me do all of that stuff."**

Larry continues to honor his mother's memory. Every April, he returns to Minneapolis to help with the annual benefit for the Carol Fitzgerald Memorial Fund, an organization established by his father shortly after his mother died. The organization helps raise money for the three causes that were closest to Larry's mother's heart: breast cancer awareness, HIV and AIDS prevention, and the education of minority youth. Of all Larry's accomplishments, his work for these causes would probably make Carol proudest of all.

The Father of American Football

Walter Chauncey Camp (1859–1925) is recognized as one of the giants of American football. His contributions helped the game develop its own identity distinct from the English game of rugby.

Camp was born in New Britain, Connecticut. He was an outstanding athlete as a young man, competing in swimming, running, and tennis, as well as football. He played at Yale University from 1877 to 1882, serving as captain of the football team for three of those years. In those days, the captain coached the team. During his time at Yale, Camp's teams produced a record of 25 wins, one defeat, and six ties.

While at Yale, Camp became a member of the Intercollegiate Football Association. At the time, the Intercollegiate Football Association was the ruling organization for the sport, and American football was very similar to rugby. Beginning in 1880, the organization accepted many new ideas that Camp proposed to improve the game. In rugby, play began when players from both teams gathered around the ball in a "scrum" and tried to kick it back to a teammate. Camp proposed the idea of a scrimmage, in which the ball is given to one team, and play begins when

Walter Camp, seen here in 1878 or 1879, is considered the "Father of American Football." Camp devised rules and innovations that distinguished football from the game of rugby, including the line of scrimmage, the quarterback position, and the first down.

the ball is snapped. To prevent one team from retaining possession for an unlimited amount of time—leading to boring, scoreless tied games—Camp proposed another rule. This would force a team to give up the ball if it did not move the ball forward a specific distance in a set number of plays, or downs.

Camp also invented a new scoring system; the rule limiting the number of players to 11 on a side; the quarterback position; the names for the other positions on a football team; and other features of strategy that helped make football more interesting to watch. His innovations helped increase the popularity of the game.

In spite of holding a full-time job at the New Haven Clock Company, Camp still found time to write numerous books and articles about football. In addition, from 1889 through 1897, Camp joined forces with sports columnist Caspar Whitney to select what is recognized as the first All-American teams.

As a result of this work, Walter Camp became known as the "Father of American Football." For his numerous contributions to the game, he was inducted into the National Football Foundation's College Football Hall of Fame as part of its first class in 1951.

(Go back to page 9.)

Fred Biletnikoff

The Fred Biletnikoff Award is named in honor of a former All-Pro wide receiver. Born in Erie, Pennsylvania, in 1943, Biletnikoff was a college football star for the Florida State University Seminoles, and he was an All-American in 1964. He ended his college career in spectacular fashion. Playing against the University of Oklahoma in the Gator Bowl, Biletnikoff helped the Seminoles to victory with four touchdown catches.

The Oakland Raiders **drafted** Biletnikoff with the second overall pick in the 1965 NFL draft. Although he did not get a chance to play regularly until 1967, Biletnikoff made the most of his opportunity and kept his place as a starter until he retired in 1978. Biletnikoff earned All-Pro honors in 1972. He played in two Super Bowls and was named Most Valuable Player (MVP) in the Raiders' 32-14 win over the Minnesota Vikings in Super Bowl XI.

At the time he retired, Biletnikoff's total of 589 receptions placed him fourth on the all-time list. The catches were good for 8,974 yards and 76 touchdowns. In 1988, Biletnikoff was inducted into the National Football League Hall of Fame. Three years later, he was inducted into the College Football Hall of Fame. In 1994, the Tallahassee Quarterback Club created the Biletnikoff Award, which is presented each year to the best receiver in college football.

(Go back to page 9.)

The *Minnesota Spokesman-Recorder*

Larry Fitzgerald Sr. has been a sports editor and columnist for the *Minnesota Spokesman-Recorder* for more than twenty years. The *Spokesman-Recorder* is the oldest minority-owned newspaper in the state, with a history that dates back to 1934. That year, Cecil E. Newman founded both the *Minneapolis Spokesman* and the *St. Paul Recorder*.

Newman was an African-American from Kansas City, Missouri. At the time he founded his newspapers, Newman was 31 years old. As a youngster, he sold newspapers. Newman gained experience in the newspaper business when he accepted an office job with the *Kansas City Call*, a local African-American publication. After moving to Minneapolis, he founded the *Twin Cities Herald* in 1927. Five years later, he published the weekly *Timely Digest* prior to founding the *Spokesman*. He remained owner and publisher of the paper until his death in 1976.

The *Minneapolis Spokesman* and the *St. Paul Recorder* merged in 2000 to form the *Minnesota Spokesman-Recorder*. Today, the paper has a circulation of approximately 60,000. It is owned and operated by Tracey L. Williams, who is Newman's granddaughter.

(Go back to page 11.) ◀◀

The First All-America Team

Credit for selecting the first college football All-America team goes to sports columnist Caspar W. Whitney. Whitney was part owner of *The Week's Sport* magazine. In 1889, he identified the players he believed to be the best at their respective positions. (It is possible that Walter Camp helped him make the selections, but the team was published under Whitney's name.) He called the group the "All-America Team." The name was somewhat misleading because the players he selected were from just three schools, all in the East. The first All-America team was composed of the following:

- "Snake" Ames, Princeton (Back)
- Roscoe H. Channing Jr., Princeton (Back)
- Hector Cowan, Princeton (Tackle)
- John Cranston, Harvard (Guard)
- Arthur Cumnock, Harvard (End)
- William J. George, Princeton (Center)

- Charles O. Gill, Yale (Tackle)
- William "Pudge" Heffelfinger, Yale (Guard)
- James T. Lee, Harvard (Back)
- Edgar Allen Poe, Princeton (Back)
- Amos Alonzo Stagg, Yale (End)

Of the eleven players selected by Whitney, four—Ames, Cowan, Heffelfinger, and Stagg—were eventually elected to the College Football Hall of Fame. Ames was one of the first fast, shifty, exciting runners that have helped make football so popular. Nicknamed "Snake" because of his winding runs, Ames holds the unofficial college football career scoring record. In addition, some people credit him with inventing the spiral punt.

Cowan was a 189-pound lineman in a time when linemen often carried the ball. He scored 79 touchdowns in his five-year career at Princeton. As captain of the team, he was one of the first to use a system of calling plays by number.

Heffelfinger was one of the biggest players of his time. Rather than just **blocking** opposing players, he would often block specifically for the runner carrying the ball. Heffelfinger may be best known as the first player who was paid to play football. He received $500 from the Duquesne Athletic Club of Pittsburgh for an 1892 game against the Allegheny Athletic Association team.

In his 57-year coaching career, Stagg made many contributions to football. He introduced the tackling dummy, the huddle, the lateral pass, the reverse and man-in-motion plays, the quick kick, and uniform numbers. Stagg is one of the few men elected to the College Football Hall of Fame as both a player and a coach. In addition, he is also credited with inventing the batting cage in which baseball players practice.

(Go back to page 13.) ◀◀

William "Pudge" Heffelfinger, pictured in his Yale sweater, circa 1889. Heffelfinger is considered the first professional football player: he received $500 to play in an 1892 game for the Duquesne Athletic Club.

Pittsburgh Panthers in the NFL

When the Arizona Cardinals selected Larry Fitzgerald with the third overall pick in the 2004 NFL draft, he became the 21st University of Pittsburgh Panther chosen in the first round of the draft. Only Tony Dorsett, who was picked second by the Dallas Cowboys in 1977, and Bill Fralic, who was picked second by the Atlanta Falcons in 1985, were selected earlier than Larry.

The first Panther ever picked in the NFL draft was tackle Ave Daniell, who was picked in the second round in 1937. Known as "Li'l Abner," Daniell lasted just one season in the NFL, during which he played for both the Green Bay Packers and the old Brooklyn Dodgers (no connection to the baseball team). The following year, back Frank Patrick became the first Panther drafted by the Cardinals' franchise, which was based in Chicago at the time.

Twelve Panthers were selected in the draft in 1981. Three of them—Hugh Green, Randy McMillan, and Mark May—were picked in the first round. The only other time three Panthers were picked in the first round of the draft was 1983, when Jim Covert, Tim Lewis, and Dan Marino were chosen. Marino is the most recent Panther to be inducted into the Pro Football Hall of Fame. He entered in 2005, joining Joe Schmidt (1973), Mike Ditka (1988), and Tony Dorsett (1994).

(Go back to page 19.) ◀◀

Head Coach Dennis Green

By the time Larry Fitzgerald joined the Arizona Cardinals in 2004, Dennis Green had established a reputation as one of the top coaches in the National Football League. From 1992 through 2000, he was the most successful coach in the NFL. As head coach of the Minnesota Vikings, he had a record of 92 wins versus just 52 losses for a winning percentage of .639. Green's 15-1 record with the Vikings in 1998 is one of the best records of any team in the history of the league. It earned him Coach of the Year honors from *Sports Illustrated* magazine.

Green played college football at the University of Iowa, where he was a tailback and flanker. After graduating from Iowa in 1971, he played one year of professional football with the British Columbia Lions of the Canadian Football League. Green then became a coach. He gained valuable experience as an assistant coach at the University of Iowa, the University of Dayton, and Stanford University.

In 1981, Green became the second African-American head coach in Division I-A history when he took the job at Northwestern University. He was named the Big Ten

In 10 years as head coach of the Minnesota Vikings, Dennis Green compiled an impressive record of 97-62. His three-year tenure with the Arizona Cardinals, however, produced a dismal 16-32 record.

Conference Coach of the Year the next season. In 1985, Green left college football to coach in the NFL. Green worked as running-backs coach for the San Francisco 49ers under head coach Bill Walsh. In 1989, Green returned to college football as head coach for Stanford University. He remained at Stanford until he got the job as coach of the Minnesota Vikings on January 10, 1992. That year, Green became the third African-American head coach in NFL history. (Go back to page 22.) ◀◀

NFL Football Around the World

More than 100,000 fans packed Mexico City's gigantic Azteca Stadium for a 2005 matchup between the Arizona Cardinals and the San Francisco 49ers on October 2, 2005.

On October 2, 2005, the Arizona Cardinals played the San Francisco 49ers in an early season matchup between two teams with losing records. Played in Azteca Stadium in Mexico City, Mexico, the game was the first regular-season NFL game ever played outside the United States. The game also set a record for attendance at an NFL game, with 103,467 fans in the stadium. The league's previous attendance record had been set 48 years before.

In the early part of the game, the 49ers took the lead. Among the highlights of the game, however, was an acrobatic catch by Larry Fitzgerald just before halftime. Larry's catch brought the Cardinals within a few points of the 49ers, and the Cardinals took over the game in the second half. The Arizona Cardinals won the game, 31-14.

NFL commissioner Paul Tagliabue was pleased with the way Mexican fans received the game. He said the league would consider playing future games in the country. The NFL brought American football to England in 2007 and 2008. In 2007, the New York Giants beat the Miami Dolphins, 13-10, in London's Wembley Stadium. The next year, the San Diego Chargers played the New Orleans Saints in the same stadium. (Go back to page 27.) ◀◀

Football Injuries

Because of the violent nature of their sport, football players can be injured in many ways. Many football injuries are not serious enough to keep a player out of a game, but others can be life threatening.

Concussions are arguably the most dangerous of all injuries that can happen in football. A concussion can occur when a player suffers a blow to the head. The blow can cause the brain to hit the inside of the skull, leading to bruising of the brain and injury to the nerves. Symptoms can include dizziness, confusion, or loss of consciousness. Concussions are classified as Grade I, Grade II, or Grade III, ranging in severity from least to most serious. Several football players, including Dallas Cowboys Hall of Fame quarterback Roger Staubach, have retired early as a result of multiple concussions.

A stinger is a common football injury that results when a player receives a hit to his head or shoulder. The hit compresses the nerves coming out of the spine, causing a burning, tingling, or weak feeling in the arm. Also called "burners," stingers are usually temporary.

Many football players injure their shoulders. When the bone of the upper arm pops out of its socket, the shoulder has been dislocated. When the ligaments connecting the bones in the shoulder are stretched or torn, the shoulder has been separated. These injuries vary in severity. Recovery time can be as little as a few days or as long as several months.

Knee injuries are probably the most common type of football injury. Bones of the knee can be fractured when one player hits another. The ligaments that hold the bones together at the knee joint—particularly the anterior cruciate ligament (ACL)—can be easily stretched or torn when the knee is forcefully twisted while the foot is in contact with the ground. An audible pop can often be heard when the ACL is torn. Repairing or replacing a torn ACL requires surgery.

Less serious football injuries include ankle sprains and turf toe. Ankle sprains occur when ligaments in the ankle joint are stretched. Turf toe is caused by jamming the foot into the ground. This injury can result in irritation and swelling around the base of the toe. Although painful, both ankle sprains and turf toe usually do not require surgery or long periods of inactivity.

(Go back to page 32.) ◀◀

The Receptions Record

Catching 100 passes in a season is a remarkable achievement for any player. The NFL record for the number of passes caught in one season was set by Marvin Harrison of the Indianapolis Colts in 2002, when he made 143 receptions. That year, Harrison had six games with ten or more catches. He exceeded 100 yards receiving in ten different games and totaled 1,722 yards for the year. Harrison broke the previous record for receptions, held by Herman Moore, by 20. Moore caught 123 passes for the Detroit Lions in 1995.

No accurate records were kept for the most passes received in the seasons from 1920 to 1931. The first recognized leader in receptions in NFL history was Ray Flaherty of the New York Giants. Flaherty recorded 21 in the 1932 season. His single-season record was surpassed

Wide receiver Marvin Harrison of the Indianapolis Colts holds the NFL record for most receptions in a single season. In 2002, Harrison caught 143 passes—breaking the previous mark by 20.

several times within the next decade. The most dominant figure during those years was Don Hutson of the Green Bay Packers. Hutson set new records four times, catching 34 passes in 1936, 41 the next year, 58 in 1941, and 74 in 1942. Hutson—who eventually made the NFL Hall of Fame—led the league in receptions eight times. Hutson's record of 74 receptions stood until the Los Angeles Rams' Tom Fears caught 77 passes in 1949. Fears beat his own record by catching 84 passes the next year.

Fears's record stood until 1960, when Lionel Taylor of the Denver Broncos caught 92 passes. Taylor was also the first receiver to reach triple digits in catches for a season, catching exactly 100 passes in 1961. The next receiver to catch 100 passes was Charley Hennigan of the Houston Oilers. Hennigan edged past Taylor with 101 catches in 1964. His record stood for 20 years.

In 1984, Art Monk caught 106 passes for the Washington Redskins. That record lasted until 1992. It was broken in each of the next four years. Sterling Sharpe caught 108 passes in 1992 and 112 in 1993. Cris Carter caught 122 passes in 1994, and Herman Moore caught 123 passes in 1995. The same year that Moore set his record, Carter and Jerry Rice each caught 122. Rice is the career leader in receptions with 1,549. His catches gained a total of 22,895 yards.

(Go back to page 41.)

The Ollie Matson Trade

Trading a top player like Larry Fitzgerald would have been a major deal. It would not, however, have been the biggest trade in Cardinals history. The trade that sent star running back Ollie Matson to the then-Los Angeles Rams after the 1958 season would still have been bigger.

Matson was an All-America running back for the University of San Francisco in 1951. That year, he led the nation in rushing yardage and touchdowns, and finished ninth in the voting for the Heisman Trophy. He also won silver and bronze medals in track and field at the 1952 Summer Olympics held in Helsinki, Finland. In 1952, Matson was drafted by the then-Chicago Cardinals with the first overall pick in the NFL draft. Matson shared Rookie of the Year honors that season, and he would go on to have a 14-year career in the league.

Following the 1958 season, the Cardinals traded Matson to the Rams in exchange for eight players, including tackle Ken Panfil, end John Tracey, tackle Frank Fuller, defensive end Glenn Holtzman, defensive tackle Art Hauser, fullback Larry Hickman, and halfback Don Brown. The big trade, however, proved to be a failure for both sides. Matson had only one more year in which he gained more than 500 yards. None of the players traded to the Cardinals ever became stars.

(Go back to page 42.)

1983 Larry Darnell Fitzgerald Jr. is born on August 31 in Minneapolis, Minnesota.

2000 Larry becomes ball boy for the Minnesota Vikings.

2001 Larry transfers from the Academy of Holy Angels in Richfield, Minnesota, to Valley Forge Military Academy in Wayne, Pennsylvania.

2002 Larry graduates from Valley Forge Military Academy and begins his freshman year at the University of Pittsburgh.

Larry is named to the All-Big East team.

2003 Larry's mother dies of cancer on April 10.

Larry earns All-America honors as a sophomore.

Larry is named E.C.A.C. Division I-A Player of the Year and Touchdown Club of Columbus Player of the Year.

Larry wins the Biletnikoff Award and the Walter Camp Award.

Larry finishes second in voting for the Heisman Trophy.

2004 Larry is selected by the Arizona Cardinals with the third overall pick in the NFL draft.

Larry signs a six-year contract with the Cardinals.

Larry leads the Cardinals with 58 receptions for 780 yards.

2005 Larry ties for the NFL lead in receptions with 103.

Larry leads the Cardinals with 1,409 yards receiving.

Larry is named to the Pro Bowl as a reserve.

2006 Larry has 69 receptions for 946 yards in spite of missing three games with an injury.

2007 Larry leads the Cardinals with 100 receptions and 1,409 yards.

Larry is named to the Pro Bowl as a starter.

2008 Larry signs a new four-year, $40 million contract with the Cardinals.

Career Statistics

Year	Team	G	Rec.	Yds.	Avg.	Lng.	TD
2004	Arizona	16	58	780	13.4	48	8
2005	Arizona	16	103	1,409	13.7	47	10
2006	Arizona	13	69	946	13.7	57	6
2007	Arizona	15	100	1,409	14.1	48	10
TOTAL		60	330	4,544	13.8	57	34

Team Records
Most receptions, single season: 103 (2005)

Awards
2002   All-Big East Team

2003   Unanimous All-America
E.C.A.C. Division I-A Player of the Year
Biletnikoff Award winner
Walter Camp Award winner
Touchdown Club of Columbus Player of the Year
Heisman Trophy runner-up

2005   NFL Pro Bowl

2007   NFL Pro Bowl

Books

Carroll, Bob. *Total Football II*. New York: HarperCollins, 1999.

Editors at the NFL. *2007 NFL Record & Fact Book*. New York: NFL, 2007.

Gilbert, Sara. *The History of the Arizona Cardinals*. Mankato, MN: Creative Education, 2005.

Nichols, John. *Arizona Cardinals*. Mankato, MN: Creative Education, 2000.

Walters, John. *NFC West: The Arizona Cardinals, the St. Louis Rams, the San Francisco 49ers, and the Seattle Seahawks*. Mankato, MN: Child's World, 2003.

Web Sites

http://www.azcardinals.com/

> The official Web site of the Arizona Cardinals includes statistics, columns, team news, ticket information, history, and more.

http://www.larry-fitzgerald.com/

> The official Web site of Larry Fitzgerald Sr., sports editor and columnist of the *Minnesota Spokesman-Reporter*, includes sports news and articles.

http://www.larry-fitzgerald.com/jr/

> The official Web site of Larry Fitzgerald Jr. includes news about Larry, pictures of him playing, and information about the Carol Fitzgerald Memorial Fund.

http://www.nfl.com/

> The official Web site of the National Football League includes information about all teams in the league and statistics.

http://www.nfl.com/players/larryfitzgerald/profile?id=FIT437493

> Larry Fitzgerald's page on the National Football League Web site includes game and career statistics.

http://www.pro-football-reference.com/

> This Web site provides a wealth of pro football statistics and resources on players, teams, and coaches, as well as NFL trivia.

blocking—getting in the way of opponents to prevent them from tackling a passer or ball carrier.

draft—in professional sports, the system by which a team gains exclusive rights to negotiate a contract with a player coming out of college.

end zone—the ten-yard-deep area between the goal line and the end line.

flea-flicker—a tricky play run by an offense in order to deceive the defense.

free agent—a professional athlete who is not under contract to any team.

hamstring—one of the muscles at the back of the thigh.

overtime—an extension of playing time to decide a winner when a score is tied.

pass interference—illegally getting in the way of a player's attempt to catch a pass.

playoffs—in professional football, games played by top teams after the regular season to determine which two teams will play in the Super Bowl.

Pro Bowl—in the NFL, the game played between the all-star teams of the National Football Conference and the American Football Conference that occurs after the Super Bowl.

quarterback—the player on a football team who tells the team what play they are running and moves the ball to a running back or receiver after the snap.

reception—in football, a forward pass that is caught by a member of the offensive team.

rookie—a first-year player on a team.

sack—in football, to tackle the quarterback behind the line of scrimmage, resulting in a loss of yardage.

safety—on a football team's defensive team, one of the defensive backs who generally lines up farthest from the line of scrimmage.

touchdown—a score of six points made by carrying the ball across the opponent's goal line.

page 6 "I've dedicated the rest of . . . " Joe Bendel, "Dorsett Boosting Fitzgerald's Heisman Hopes," *Pittsburgh Tribune-Review* (November 27, 2003). http://www.pittsburghlive.com/x/pittsburghtrib/s_167175.html

page 6 "I thought about her quite . . . " Doug Frattallone, "Football & Faith," *Minnesota SCORE*. http://www.minnesotascore.com/articles/faith.html

page 7 "This guy is really unbelievable . . . " "Larry Fitzgerald Earns Rave Midseason Reviews," pittsburghpanthers.cstv.com (October 16, 2003). http://pittsburghpanthers.cstv.com/sports/m-footbl/spec-rel/101603aaa.html

page 12 "Just watching guys like Cris . . . " Jon Krawczynski, "Healthy Fitzgerald Ready to Come Home," Associated Press (November 23, 2006). http://www.rockymountainnews.com/drmn/nfl/article/0,2777,DRMN_23918_5164244,00.html

page 12 "I hit the ball hard . . . " Tim Layden, "So Good, Too Soon?" *Sports Illustrated* (December 8, 2003). http://vault.sportsillustrated.cnn.com/vault/article/magazine/MAG1030785/index.htm

page 15 "He was so overwhelmed with . . . " Layden, "So Good, Too Soon?"

page 16 "He not only showed people . . . " Joe Bendel, "Harris: Fitzgerald Is Ready for NFL," *Pittsburgh Tribune-Review* (December 20, 2003). http://www.pittsburghlive.com/x/pittsburghtrib/s_170928.html

page 18 "It is perfectly clear that . . . " Damon Hack, "NFL Grants Eligibility to Fitzgerald, Pitt Receiver," *The New York Times* (May 26, 2008). http://query.nytimes.com/gst/fullpage.html?res=9C0DE2DF113BF935A35751C0A9629C8B63

page 20 "With the third pick of . . . " Larry Fitzgerald Sr., "Larry Fitzgerald Jr. Drafted No 1 by Arizona Cardinals!" *Minnesota Spokesman-Recorder* (April 29, 2004). http://www.larry-fitzgerald.com/articles/Larry-Fitzgerald-Jr-drafted-No-1-by-Arizona-Cardinals.htm

page 21 "To be able to come . . . " Fitzgerald, "Larry Fitzgerald Jr. Drafted No 1 by Arizona Cardinals!"

page 25 "They threw me in the . . . " Judy Battista, "Rookies Range from Wait and See, to Watch Them Go," *The New York Times* (November 12, 2004). http://www.nytimes.com/2004/11/12/sports/football/12nfl.html

page 29 "I'm always in their ear . . . " Kate Brandt, "Fitz Enjoying Time In Hawaii," azcardinals.com (February 9, 2006). http://www.azcardinals.com/news/detail.php?PRKey=744

page 32 "This is my third year . . . " Krawczynski, "Healthy Fitzgerald Ready to Come Home."

page 35 "In the final analysis, when . . . " Kent Somers, "Cardinals Fire Green After Three Losing Seasons in the Desert," *The Arizona Republic* (January 1, 2007). http://www.usatoday.com/sports/football/nfl/cards/2007-01-01-green-firing_x.htm

page 35 "Dennis is a good coach . . . " Jim Gintonio, "Don't Put All the Blame on Green, Cardinals Players Say," *The Arizona Republic* (January 1, 2007). http://www.usatoday.com/sports/football/nfl/cards/2007-01-01-green-reaction_x.htm

page 38 "We're not going to change . . . " Len Pasquarelli, "Cardinals a Team on the Rise," *ESPN.com* (March 12, 2007). http://sports.espn.go.com/nfl/columns/story?columnist=pasquarelli_len&id=2795359

page 38 "[They are] high-character . . . " "Fitzgerald Is Head and Shoulders Above the Crowd," Associated Press

(December 2, 2007). http://www.nytimes.com/2007/12/02/sports/football/02cardinals.html?ex=1354251600&en=05880ad81e643091&ei=5088&partner=rssnyt&emc=rss

page 45 "That's one of the first . . . " Darren Urban, "Rodgers-Cromartie Is Top Pick," azcardinals.com (April 26, 2008). http://www.azcardinals.com/news/detail.php?PRKey=2331

page 45 "My mom wouldn't want me . . . " Mark Craig, "Vikings: Minneapolis Native Larry Fitzgerald Still a Mama's Boy," *Star Tribune* (November 23, 2006). http://www.startribune.com/sports/vikings/11703991.html

Numbers in **bold italics** refer to captions.

John F. Grabowski is a teacher and freelance writer from Staten Island, New York. His published work includes 50 books, a nationally syndicated sports column, consultation on several math textbooks, dozens of articles for newspapers, magazines, and the programs of professional sports teams, and comedy material sold to Jay Leno, Joan Rivers, Yakov Smirnoff, and numerous other comics.

PICTURE CREDITS